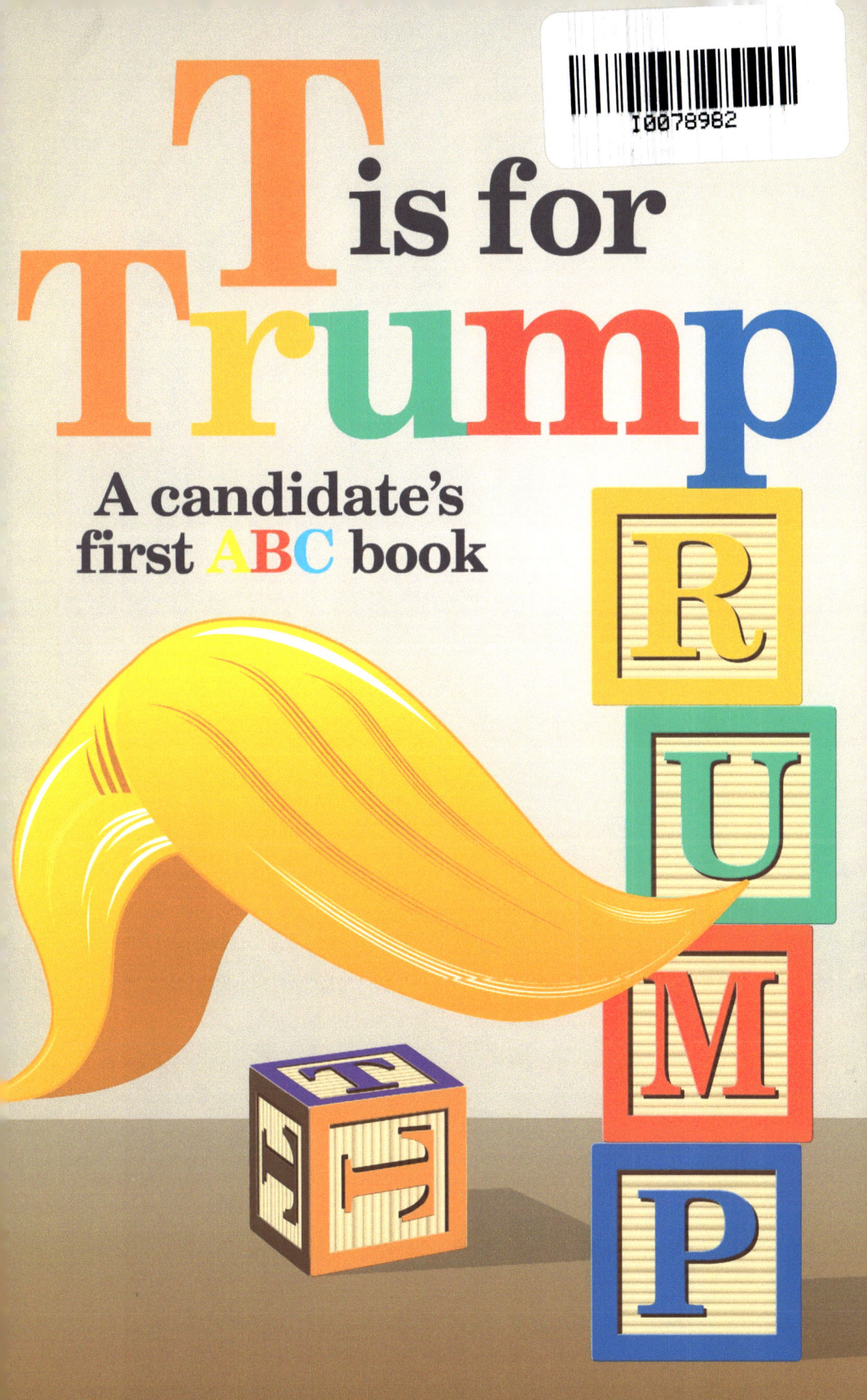

T is for

Copyright © 2016 by G. Thomas Mandel

All rights reserved. This book or any portion thereof may not be reproduced or used in any manner whatsoever without the express written permission of the publisher except for the use of brief quotations in a book review.

Printed in the United States of America

First Printing, 2016

ISBN 978-0692756867

 A Ridge Street Book

www.TisforTrump.com   TisforTrump@gmail.com

Trump

A candidate's first ABC book

Written and illustrated by G. Thomas Mandel

A is for

ap·pren·tice (ə-prĕn′tis)

n.

Apprentice

1. a talentless celebrity hack.
Syns: *see lackey, sycophant, lickspittle.*

B is for

blood (blŭd)
n.

C is for

comb·o·ver (cōm′ō-vər′)

n.

Combover

Syns: *see bald, hairless, bald as a cue ball.*

D is for

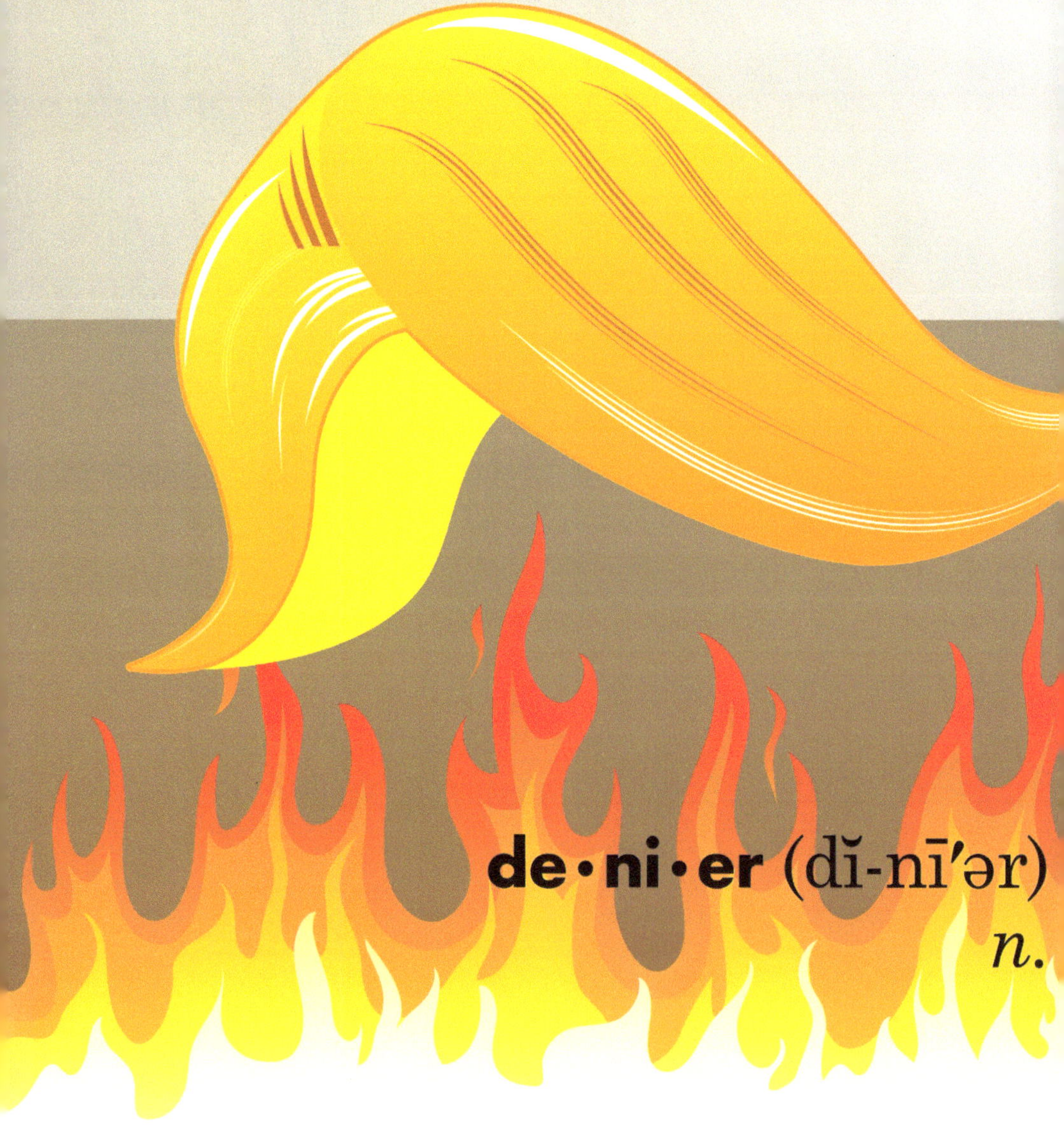

de•ni•er (dĭ-nī′ər)

n.

E is for

e·go (ē′gō)
n.

1. the faculty of the brain that allows an unqualified individual to run for president.

F is for

fin·ger (fĭng′gər)
n.

G is for

God (gŏd)
n.

God

1. the creator of the universe, a supreme being that clearly has a sense of humor.

Huge

1. something small that is said to be enormous, *e.g.*, a small crowd of supporters.

I is for

I·van·a, I·van·ka
(ī-vŏn′ə, ī-vŏn′kə)
n.

J is for

judge (jŭj)
n.

Judge

1. a member of the judiciary who makes decisions solely based on ethnic heritage.

K is for

Ken·ya (kĕn′ye, kēn′-)

n.

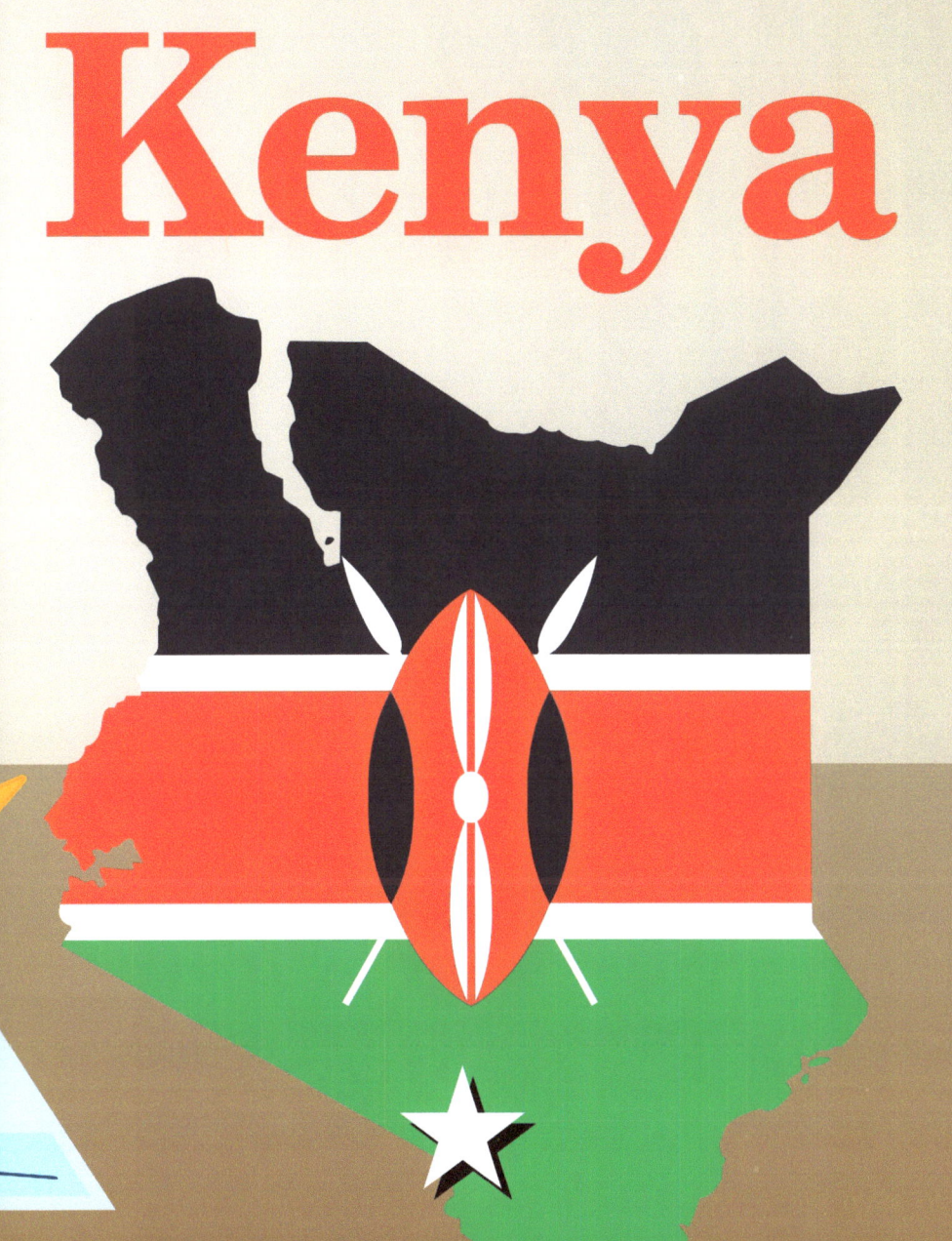

Kenya

1. the birthplace of Barack Obama, 44th President of the United States.

L is for

li•ar (lī'ər)

n.

M is for

mar·la, mel·an·ia
(mär′lə, mĕ-län′yə)
n.

Marla Melania

1. generic term for wife, ex-wife, mistress or daughter, esp. of Eastern European descent.

O is for

o·range (ôr′ĭnj, ŏr′)
adj.

Orange

1. a skin or hair color not normally found in nature.

P is for

pres•i•dent (prĕz′ĭ-dənt)

n.

President

1. *Democrat.* A high elected official. **2.** *Republican.* A reality show host.

Quality

1. without any distinction or value. **Syns:** *see Trump brand, Trump property.*

Racist

Biggest Bigot Ever!

1. a candidate who ignores the endorsement of white supremacist groups.

S is for

steak (stāk)

n.

Steak

1. a cut of beef known primarily for its tough, leathery exterior and mushy interior.

T is for

Trump (trŭmp) *n.*

1. *(vulgar)* an obscenity. **Syns:** *see ass, asswipe, butthead.*

U is for

u·ni·ver·si·ty
(yōō'-nə-vûr'sĭ-tē)
n.

University

1. a fraudulent enterprise.
Syns: *see diploma mill, con, scam.*

Vulgar

1. the normal speech, behavior and mannerisms of certain political candidates.

wall (wôl) *n.*

Wall

1. A structure dividing two sovereign nations, inexplicably paid for by the poorer nation.

X is for

xen·o·phobe (zĕn′ə-fōb′)

n.

Xenophobe

1. an individual who is terrified by foreigners, especially Muslims.

You're Fired

1. a phrase spoken to a celebrity host when his reality show is cancelled.

Z is for

zil·lion·aire (zĭl′yə-nâr′) *n.*

Zillionaire

1. *Mythology.* An individual so wealthy that he no longer cares about money or power.

For Nanny Rose, who taught me to read.

Special thanks to the members of the
T is for Trump Brain Trust
...you know who you are.

www.ingramcontent.com/pod-product-compliance
Lightning Source LLC
Chambersburg PA
CBHW041524090426
42737CB00038B/115